Kid's Box for Ecuador

Student's Book 1B

Caroline Nixon & Michael Tomlinson

Ecuadorian CLIL content by Kate Cory-Wright and Jill Hadfield

CAMBRIDGE
UNIVERSITY PRESS

Thanks and Acknowledgments

Authors' thanks

Many thanks to everyone at Cambridge University Press and in particular to:

Rosemary Bradley for supervising the whole project and for her keen editorial eye;
Emily Hird for her energy, enthusiasm, and enormous organizational capacity;
Colin Sage for his hard work, good ideas, and helpful suggestions;
Claire Appleyard for her editorial contribution.

Many thanks to Karen Elliot for her expertise and enthusiasm in the writing of the Phonics sections.

We would also like to thank all our pupils and colleagues at Star English, El Palmar, Murcia, and especially Jim Kelly and Julie Woodman for their help and suggestions at various stages of the project.

Dedications

I would like to dedicate this book to the women who have been my pillars of strength: Milagros Marín, Sara de Alba, Elia Navarro, and Maricarmen Balsalobre - CN

To Paloma, for her love, encouragement, and unwavering support. Thanks. - MT

The Authors and Publishers would like to thank the following teachers for their help in reviewing the material and for the invaluable feedback they provided:

Luciana Pittondo, Soledad Gimenez, Argentina; Gan Ping, Zou Yang, China; Keily Duran, Colombia; Elvia Gutierrez Reyes, Yadira Hernandez, Mexico; Rachel Lunan, Russia; Lorraine Mealing, Sharon Hopkins, Spain; Inci Kartal, Turkey.

The authors and publishers would like to thank the following consultants for their invaluable feedback:

Coralyn Bradshaw, Pippa Mayfield, Hilary Ratcliff, Melanie Williams.

We would also like to thank all the teachers who allowed us to observe their classes and who gave up their invaluable time for interviews and focus groups.

The authors and publishers acknowledge the following sources of copyright material and are grateful for the permissions granted. While every effort has been made, it has not always been possible to identify the sources of all the material used or to trace all copyright holders. If any omissions are brought to our notice, we will be happy to include the appropriate acknowledgments on reprinting.

t = top, c = centre, b = below, l = left, r = right.

p. 60 (tl): Shutterstock.com/Gualtiero Boffi; p. 60 (tr, bc): Shutterstock/Eric Isselee; p. 60 (bl): Shutterstock/Volodymyr Krasyuk; p. 60 (br): Shutterstock/ Ekaterina V. Borisova; p. 60 (tc): Shutterstock/defpicture; p. 61 (t): Thinkstock; p. 61a (tl): Getty Images/David Hiser/The Image Bank; p. 61a (tc): Getty Images/Juergen Ritterbach/DigitalVision; p. 61a (tr): Getty Images/Lilly Husbands; p. 61a (bl): Getty Images/onairda/iStock; p. 61a (bc): Getty Images/Istvan Kadar Photography/Moment; p. 61a (br): Getty Images/Ben Queenborough/Oxford Scientific; p. 61b (br): Getty Images/ Guy Edwardes/The Image Bank; p. 61b (tr): Getty Images/ KalypsoWorldPhotography/iStock; p. 61b (tl): Getty Images/ Julia Davila-Lampe/Moment Open; p. 62 (l): Shutterstock/ MIMOHE; p. 62 (r): Shutterstock/Jiri Foltyn; p. 62 (cl): Shutterstock/ Jassam; p. 62 (cr): Shutterstock/Claudia Otte; p. 76 (tl): Getty Images/AFP/TORU YAMANAKA; p. 76 (cl): Alamy/©Kuttig - People; p. 76 (br): Corbis/ZUMA Press/©Brian Baer; p. 76 (bl): Corbis/©Onne van der Wal; p 76 (tr): Superstock/Juniors; p. 77 (t): Thinkstock; p. 77a (tl): Getty Images/Jupiterimages/Taxi; p. 77a (tr): Alamy/ Supparsorn Wantarnagon; p. 77a (bl): Getty Images/ Simon Watson/The Image Bank; p. 77a (br): Getty Images/ IMAGEMORE Co, Ltd.; p. 90 (tr, bl): SuperStock/Christie's Images Ltd; p. 90 (tl): Superstock/Leslie Hinrichs; p. 90 (br): Superstock/Peter Willi; p. 91 (t): Thinkstock.

We would like to thank the Crow family for the paintings Tren Volador (p. 91a) and Lluvia de manzanas (p. 91b).

Cover photography by Getty Images/pxhidalgo/iStock.

Background image on pages 61a, 61b, 77a, 77b, 91a, 91b by Getty Images/madebymarco/iStock.

Commissioned photography on pages 52, 68, 81 by Trevor Clifford Photography.

The authors and publishers are grateful to the following illustrators:

Beatrice Costamagna, c/o Pickled ink; Chris Garbutt, c/o Arena; Lucía Serrano Guerroro; Andrew Hennessey; Kelly Kennedy, c/o Sylvie Poggio; Sara Lynn, c/o Astound; Rob McKlurkan, c/o The Bright Agency; Andrew Painter; Melanie Sharp, c/o Sylvie Poggio; Marie Simpson, c/o Pickled ink; Christos Skaltsas (hyphen); Emily Skinner, c/o Graham Cameron Illustration; Lisa Smith; Gary Swift; Ando Twin, c/o Astound; Lisa Williams, c/o Sylvie Poggio.

The publishers are grateful to the following contributors:

Louise Edgeworth: art direction
Hilary Fletcher: picture research
Wild Apple Design Ltd: page design
Blooberry: additional design
Melanie Sharp: cover illustration
John Green and Tim Woolf, TEFL Audio: audio recordings
John Marshall Media, Inc. and Lisa Hutchins: audio recordings for the American English edition
Robert Lee: song writing
hyphen S.A.: publishing management, American English edition

Language summary

	Key vocabulary	Key grammar and functions	Phonics
7 Wild animals page 48	Animals: *crocodile, elephant, giraffe, hippo, monkey, snake, tiger* Body parts: *arm, foot/feet, hand, leg, tail*	They have (big mouths). They don't have (tails). Do they have (long legs)? How many (teeth) do they have?	Short vowel sound: "i" (s*i*x)
8 My clothes page 54	Clothes: *jacket, (pair of) pants, shoes, skirt, socks, T-shirt*	He/She has (red pants). He/She doesn't have (a jacket).	Short vowel sound: "o" (d*o*ll)

Marie's geography | Habitats   page 60   Natural science | Animals   page 61a

Trevor's values | Love nature   page 61

Review 5–8   page 62

	Key vocabulary	Key grammar and functions	Phonics
9 Fun time! page 64	Activities: *play soccer / basketball / tennis, play the guitar/piano, swim, ride a bike, sing, fish*	I/You/She/He can (sing). I/You/She/He can't (drive a car). What can you do? Can you (fish)?	Consonant sound: "l" (*L*i*l*y, b*l*ue)
10 At the amusement park page 70	Vehicles: *boat, bus, helicopter, motorcycle, plane, truck*	What are you doing? I'm (flying).	Short vowel sound: "u" (d*u*ck)

Marie's sports | Things for sports   page 76   Physical education | Games   page 77a

Trevor's values | Work in teams   page 77

	Key vocabulary	Key grammar and functions	Phonics
11 Our house page 78	Rooms: *bathroom, bedroom, dining room, hallway, kitchen, living room* Activities: *eat fish, watch TV, take a bath*	What's he/she doing? He's/She's (listening to music). What are they doing? They're (sitting on the couch). Is he/she (reading)? Yes, he/she is. No, he/she isn't. Verb + -ing spellings: *coloring, playing*	Initial consonant sound: "h" (*h*orse)
12 Party time! page 84	Food: *apple, banana, burger, cake, chocolate, ice cream* Activities: *make a cake*	I like (cake). I don't like (chocolate). Do you like (snakes)? Yes, I do. No, I don't.	Long vowel sound: "i_e"/"y" (bik*e*, fl*y*)

Marie's art | Fruit in paintings   page 90   Arts and crafts | Endara Crow   page 91a

Trevor's values | Keep clean   page 91

Review 9–12   page 92   Grammar reference   page GR1

Wild animals

1 🔵 CD3 Listen and point.

giraffe

elephant

crocodile

hippo

snake

monkey

tiger

2 🔵 CD3 Listen and repeat.

3 🔊 5 CD3 🤸 Say the chant. Do the actions.

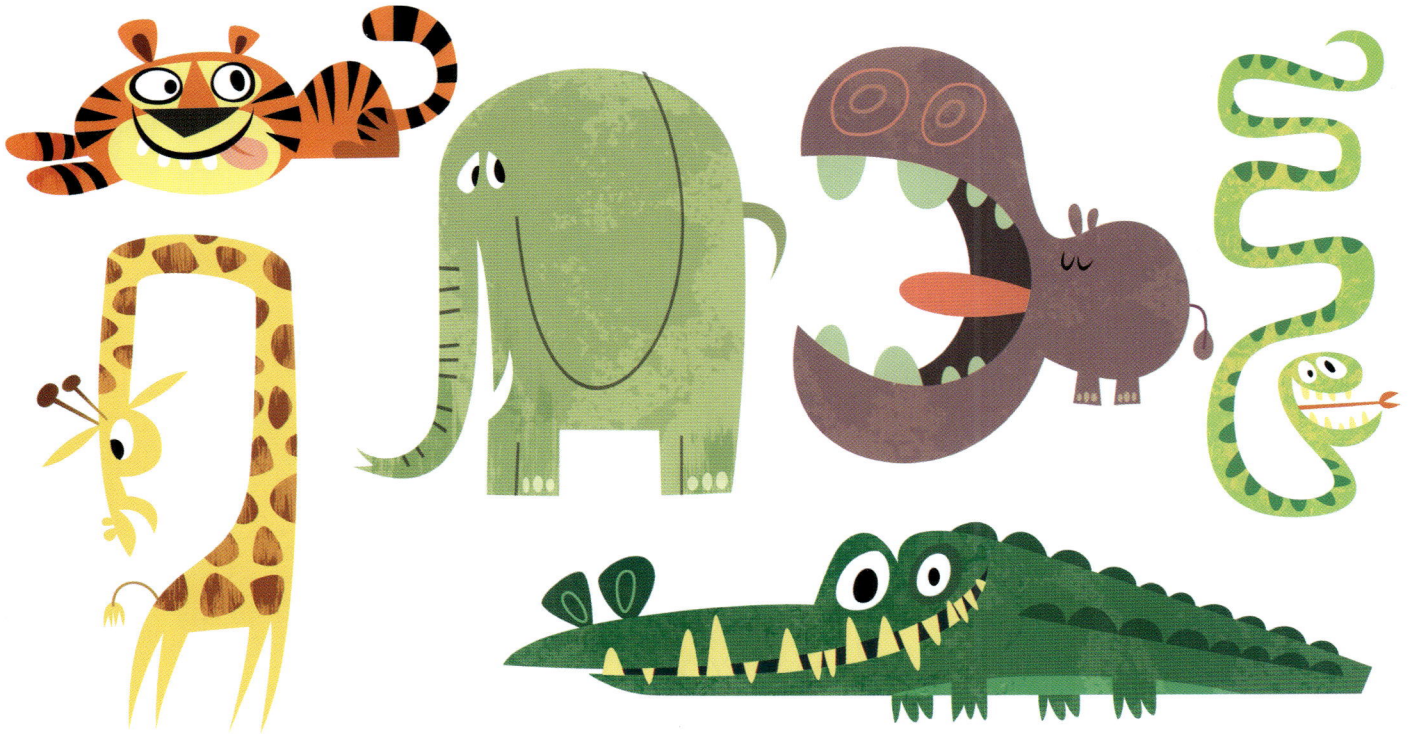

4 🔊 6 CD3 👉 Listen and point. Answer.

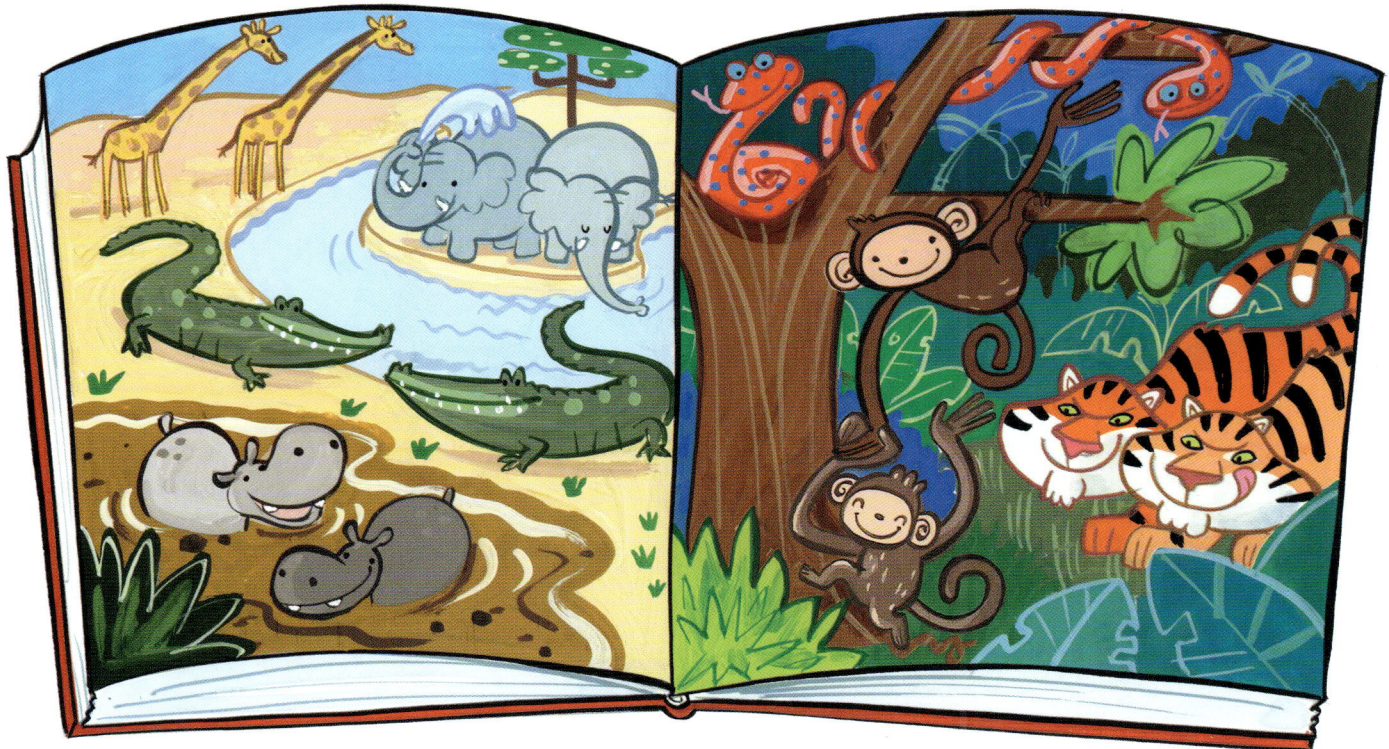

Vocabulary

crocodile elephant giraffe hippo monkey snake tiger

5 ▶ 7 CD3 Listen and point.

foot

hand

arm

leg

tail

feet

They have big ears.

6 ▶ 8 CD3 Listen and repeat.

Grammar
They have / They don't have arms / feet / hands / legs / tails.

7 🔊 CD3 10 🎵 Sing the song.

8 🧑 💬 Act it out and say.

What am I?

You're an elephant.

fish

big

Six big fish.

10 🏃💬 Play the game. Ask and answer.

Do they have small ears?

No, they don't.

big	heads, ears, feet,		short	tails, noses,
small	mouths		long	legs, arms

11 Listen to the story.

12 Act out the story.

8 My clothes

1 15 CD3 👆 Listen and point.

T-shirt

skirt

socks

shoes

jacket

pants

2 16 CD3 💬 Listen and repeat.

54

3 ▶ 18 CD3 💬 Say the chant.

4 ▶ 19 CD3 💬 Listen and say the number.

1
2
3
4

Vocabulary

jacket pants shoes skirt socks T-shirt

5 **21** CD3 Listen and point.

Does Scott have my red pants?

6 **22** CD3 Listen and repeat.

Grammar
He/She has …   He/She doesn't have …

7 **25** **CD3** 💬 Listen and correct.

8 **26** **CD3** 🎵 Sing the song.

3 🔊19 CD4 Listen to the story.

1

2

3

4

4 🔊20 CD4 💬 Listen and say the number. Act it out.

1 👂👆 Listen and point.

clap   hop   jump rope   play marbles

2 👂🤸 Listen and do the actions.

3 👤💬 Play the game. Ask and answer.

> What's the girl doing?

> She's hopping.

Language through the arts

4 💬👤 Play the game. Use a spinner.

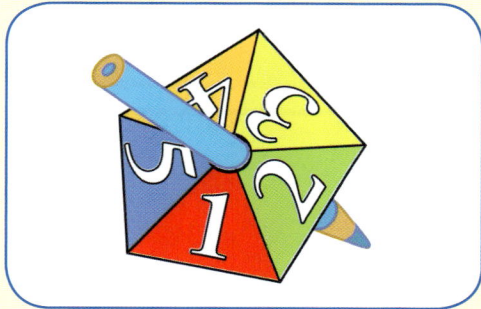

> It's your turn.

> Hop five times!

> It's my turn.

> Jump rope three times!

1

2

3

4

5

11 Our house

1 CD4 21 Listen and point.

bedroom

bathroom

living room

dining room

kitchen

hallway

2 CD4 22 Listen and repeat.

3 CD4 24 ⚬ Listen and correct.

Monty's in the bathroom.

No, he isn't. He's in the bedroom.

4 CD4 25 ⚬ Listen and answer.

Where's the computer?

It's in the kitchen.

Vocabulary

bathroom   bedroom   dining room   hallway   kitchen   living room

5 🔊 26 CD4 👂 Listen and point.

What's Scott doing?

He's drawing a picture.

6 🔊 27 CD4 💬 Listen and repeat.

Grammar

What's he/she doing?   He's/She's ...ing

7 🎵 Sing the song.

8 💬 Ask and answer.

What's Sally doing?

She's reading a book.

Where is she?

She's in the bedroom.

horse

hippo

A **h**orse and a **h**ippo in a **h**elicopter.

10 💬 **Say and guess.**

playing	driving	flying	eating
reading	playing	swimming	watching

They're eating fish.

Number four.

1

2

3

4

5

6

7

8

11 🔊 **33** Listen to the story.

12 🔊 **34** Listen and say "yes" or "no."

12 Party time!

Happy Birthday

ice cream

apple

banana

cake

burger

chocolate

2 CD4 36 Listen and repeat.

84

3 38 CD4 🗨 Say the chant.

4 39 CD4 🗨 Listen and say "yes" or "no."

Vocabulary

apple   banana   burger   cake   chocolate   ice cream   orange

I like chocolate cake.

I don't like chocolate.

Do you like Maskman cake?

Grammar

I like ...   I don't like ...   Do you like ... ?

7 🔊43 CD4 🎵Sing the song.

8 💬Ask and answer.

Do you like apples?   Yes, I do.

Do you like ice cream?   No, I don't.

like

white

bike

I like my white bike!

10 **47** CD4 💬 Read. Listen and say the name.

Sam — I like 🏀 and ⚽ , but I don't like 🏊 or 🎾 .

Sue — I don't like 🐕 or 🐎 , but I like 🐈 and 🐦 .

May — I like 👗 and 🧥 , but I don't like 👖 or 👕 .

Ben — I don't like 🍔 or 🍫 , but I like 🍦 and 🥪 .

11 🔵 **49 CD4** Listen to the story.

12 👤💬 Act out the story.

1 👀💬 Point and say the food.

1

2

3

4

2 🔊50 CD4 💬 Listen and say the number.

Vocabulary

painting   grapes   lemon   pear   watermelon

Now you!
Workbook page 90

3 🔊 51 CD4 👂 Listen and point.

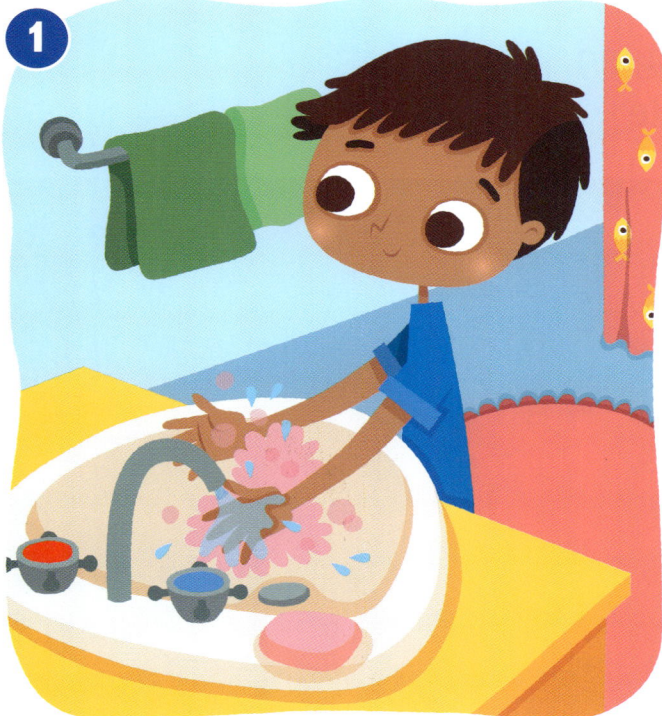

1

2

3

4 🔊 52 CD4 💬 Say the chant. Do the actions.

Vocabulary

brush your teeth   wash apples   wash your hands

1 🎧👆 Listen and point.

> apples falling flying looking
> mountains people sky train

2 🎧💬 Listen and correct.

> The mountains are gray and black.

> No. The mountains are green.

② 🔍 ✏️ **Follow the lines and write.**

| ~~bedroom~~ living room kitchen hallway |

① ② ③ ④

bedroom _

③ ✏️ **Draw your house.**

Me!

My house has

_ _ _ _ _ _ _ _ _ _ _ _ _ _ _ _

_ _ _ _ _ _ _ _ _ _ _ _ _ _ _ _

_ _ _ _ _ _ _ _ _ _ _ _ _ _ _ _

_ _ _ _ _ _ _ _ _ _ _ _ _ _ _ _

_ _ _ _ _ _ _ _ _ _ _ _ _ _ _ _

_ _ _ _ _ _ _ _ _ _ _ _ _ _ _ _

_ _ _ _ _ _ _ _ _ _ _ _ _ _ .

4 🎧 28 CD4 ✏️ **Listen and color the stars.**

①

②

③

④

⑤

⑥

5 🔍 ✏️ **Match and write.**

① She's drawing a _____picture_____ .

② He's reading a _____ .

③ She's sitting on a _____ .

④ They're listening to _____ .

⑤ He's driving a _____ .

⑥ They're playing _____ .

chair

tennis

car

book

music

picture

6 🔍✏️ **Look, read, and write.**

Where are the children?   in the _____ kitchen _____

1 What's the girl eating?   _____

2 What does the boy have?   a _____

3 What's the girl doing?   _____ to music

4 What animal can the boy see?   an _____

7 🔊 32 CD4 ✏️ Listen and circle the "h" words.

①

②

③

④

⑤

⑥

⑦

⑧

⑨

8 ✏️ Complete the sentences.

| eating | ~~listening~~ | reading | taking |

①

He's __listening__ to music.

②

She's _____ a bath.

③

He's _____ a fish.

④

She's _____ a book.

My picture dictionary

? ? ? ?	? ? ? ?	? ? ? ?
living room	bedroom	kitchen
? ? ? ?	? ? ? ?	? ? ? ?
bathroom	hallway	dining room

My star card

💬 Can you say these words?

✏️ Color the stars.

12 Party time!

1 🎵37 CD4 ✏️ Listen and color.

2 ✏️ Circle and write the words.

a	w	e	i	f	i	s	h	s
c	h	o	c	o	l	a	t	e
a	b	r	e	c	k	f	a	m
k	l	t	c	h	e	j	p	r
e	b	u	r	g	e	r	p	o
p	r	o	e	v	i	s	l	b
b	a	n	a	n	a	t	e	g
j	z	o	m	e	r	s	t	u
o	r	a	n	g	e	v	i	e

① _____ ⑤ _____

② _____ ⑥ *ice cream*

③ _____ ⑦ _____

④ _____ ⑧ _____

3 ✏️ Write the words.

1 → _cat_

2 →

3 →

4 →

4 🔍✏️ Read and complete.

young

~~eating~~

banana

cake

The small monkey's __eating__ an orange, and the big monkey has some _____. The old monkey's eating a _____, and the _____ monkey has ice cream.

5 **42** **CD4** Listen and check (✓) or put an **X**.

①  ✓  ☐  ☐  ☐

②  ☐  ☐  ☐  ☐

③  ☐  ☐  ☐  ☐

④  ☐  ☐  ☐  ☐

6 Write "like" or "don't like."

Me!

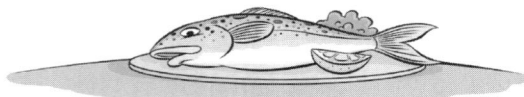

I _ _ _ _ _ _ _ _ _ _ fish.

Me!

I _ _ _ _ _ _ _ _ _ _ burgers.

Me!

I _ _ _ _ _ _ _ _ _ _ ice cream.

Me!

I _ _ _ _ _ _ _ _ _ _ apples.

7 **45** **CD4** Listen and color.

8 🔊 48 CD4 ✏️ Listen and write the words.

| bike white drive nine ~~like~~ five |

①

___like___

②

_____

③

_____

④

_____

⑤

_____

⑥

_____

9 ✏️ Check (✔) the boxes.

Name	🍎🍎	🍌	🍫	🐟	🍰	🍔🍔
Me						

💬✏️ Now ask and answer in groups.

(Do you like apples?) (Yes, I do.)

My picture dictionary ⭐

apple	banana	burger
? ? ? ?	? ? ?	? ? ? ?

cake	chocolate	ice cream
? ? ? ?	? ? ?	? ? ? ?

My star card ⭐

💬 Can you say these words?

✏️ Color the stars.

89

1 🔍✏️ **Read and circle a word.**

This is Fred Food.

His nose is a banana / an ice-cream cone.

His mouth is a fish / a burger.

His ears are apples / oranges.

His hair is grapes / lemons.

His eyes are cakes / burgers.

Now you! 2 ✏️👤 **Draw and color your Fred Food.**

Fred Food

3 🔍✏️ **Order the pictures.**

1
 2  3  1

2

3

4 🔍✏️ **Read and write.**

brushing washing washing

He's _ _ _ _ _ _ _ _ _ _
his hands.

She's _ _ _ _ _ _ _ _ _ _
her teeth.

He's _ _ _ _ _ _ _ _ _ _
his apples.

Review

1 ✏️ Check (✓) a box.

reading a book						
eating fish						
watching TV						
taking a bath						

💬✏️ Now ask and answer. Check (✓) your friend's box.

> What's the old monster doing?

> He's eating fish.

reading a book						
eating fish						
watching TV						
taking a bath						

2 ✏️ Circle the different word.

1. banana   apple   orange   (guitar)

2. truck   ice cream   train   bus

3. burger   tiger   giraffe   crocodile

4. bathroom   kitchen   bedroom   chocolate

5. motorcycle helicopter   truck   hallway

6. play   swim   bike   ride

3 🔍✏️ Read and complete. Draw.

I'm _____.

I'm at home in the kitchen. I like

_____,

but I don't like

_____.

My favorite food is

_____.

Me!

Thanks and Acknowledgments

Authors' thanks

Many thanks to everyone at Cambridge University Press and in particular to:

Rosemary Bradley for supervising the whole project and for her keen editorial eye;
Emily Hird for her energy, enthusiasm, and enormous organizational capacity;
Colin Sage for his hard work, good ideas, and helpful suggestions;
Claire Appleyard for her editorial contribution.

Many thanks to Karen Elliot for her expertise and enthusiasm in the writing of the Phonics sections.

We would also like to thank all our pupils and colleagues at Star English, El Palmar, Murcia, and especially Jim Kelly and Julie Woodman for their help and suggestions at various stages of the project.

Dedications

I would like to dedicate this book to the women who have been my pillars of strength: Milagros Marín, Sara de Alba, Elia Navarro, and Maricarmen Balsalobre - CN

To Paloma, for her love, encouragement, and unwavering support. Thanks. - MT

The Authors and Publishers would like to thank the following teachers for their help in reviewing the material and for the invaluable feedback they provided:

Luciana Pittondo, Soledad Gimenez, Argentina; Gan Ping, Zou Yang, China; Keily Duran, Colombia; Elvia Gutierrez Reyes, Yadira Hernandez, Mexico; Rachel Lunan, Russia; Lorraine Mealing, Sharon Hopkins, Spain; Inci Kartal, Turkey.

The authors and publishers would like to thank the following consultants for their invaluable feedback:

Coralyn Bradshaw, Pippa Mayfield, Hilary Ratcliff, Melanie Williams.

We would also like to thank all the teachers who allowed us to observe their classes and who gave up their invaluable time for interviews and focus groups.

The authors and publishers are grateful to the following illustrators:

Beatrice Costamagna, c/o Pickled ink; James Elston, c/o Syvlie Poggio; Chris Garbutt, c/o/ Arena; Lucía Serrano Guerroro; Andrew Hennessey; Kelly Kennedy, c/o Syvlie Poggio; Rob McKlurkan, c/o The Bright Agency; Melanie Sharp, c/o Syvlie Poggio; Marie Simpson, c/o Pickled ink; Emily Skinner, c/o Graham-Cameron Illustration; Lisa Smith; Gary Swift; Matt Ward, c/o Beehive; Lisa Williams, c/o Syvlie Poggio;

The publishers are grateful to the following contributors:

Wild Apple Design Ltd: page design
Blooberry: additional design
Lon Chan: cover design
Melanie Sharp: cover illustration
John Green and Tim Woolf, TEFL Audio: audio recordings
John Marshall Media, Inc. and Lisa Hutchins: audio recordings for the American English edition
Robert Lee: song writing
hyphen S.A.: publishing management, American English edition

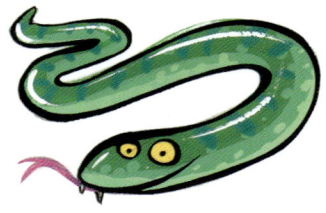

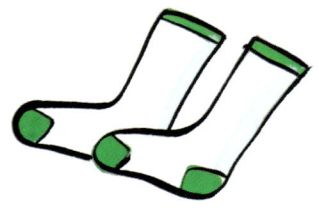